HUMPTY-DUMPTY
WILLIAM & CO.

Humpty-Dumpty sat on a wall,
Humpty-Dumpty had a great fall,
And all the king's horses
And all the king's men
Could not put Humpty-Dumpty together again!

Old Nursery Rhyme

HUMPTY-DUMPTY
WILLIAM & CO.

A POPULAR HISTORY OF TIME'S
GREATEST WAR

BY
GEORGE MAGRUDER BATTEY, Jr.

Front Cover by
LEWIS C. GREGG

Sketches by
C. J. HOLLERAN

THE DE VINNE PRESS
NEW YORK
1916

TO
MY MOTHER

FORMAL BOW

SINCE this little volume contains a good deal about the Kaiser, we are taking the liberty of sending him a copy. Far be it from us to suggest that he will laugh himself to death and thus bring the big war to an abrupt end. At the same time, we shall anxiously await the outcome; and we shall also pray that the British do not misplace the book in handling the United States mails.

So many serious things have been written about the war that we hereby cast our lot with the cartoonists and others who have attempted to make the world's burden lighter. To persons with a sense of humor we direct our humble appeal; to others we do not recommend the work, lest they should inquire about our office hours.

We do not tread upon anybody's toes maliciously. We are proud of our English and German ancestry—proud of an English ancestor who not so long ago left the Mother Country with many other steerage aristocrats, and of a German ancestor who got his start in life attending bar. We are also proud of our American friends, whether they bear the hyphen or can't bear it, and to all we would respectfully call attention to the high price of print paper and make the following request, to wit:

If the little book please you, kindly refrain from reading it a second time. Run and buy another copy!

CONTENTS

CONTENTS

SKETCHES

SPOOKS ON ST. HELENA

(IF THE ALLIES WIN)

ON a lonely isle which is generally known
  By the name of St. Helena,
In nineteen-forty browsed a gent
In a bed of lemon verbena,
Who once upon a time, 'tis said,
Built a monster funeral pyre
With the forms of first-class fighting men,
And set the world on fire.

His spine was bent, his eye was red,
His voice was strangely rasping,
And for the things he once enjoyed
This gent was wildly grasping.
He missed the fuss they made o'er him,
The epaulets of yore,
And heroes' skulls for paperweights
In the days of peasant gore.

"Crool fate hath sent me here!" he wailed,
"To spend my time alone;
I want my pipe, I want my beer—
'Tis sad to sit and moan!
My sole companion speaks no word—
He's a worthless Whifflebat—
His presence only reminds me of
The wretched place I'm at!"

The marooner heaved a pent-up sigh
As he pondered what he'd said;
(Too late to eat them unkind words—
The Whifflebat was dead!)
"It can't be helped!" the master croaked,
"Time changes everything,
And I'd like to know when the jig is up
For a broken-down old king!"

A shadow-man from somewhere came
And perched on a tall verbena;
"Did you know," he said, "that your Uncle Nap
Once rusted on St. Helena?"
"Mein Gott, Uncle Nap, I am pleased to see
You here!" was the quick reply;
"Will you do me a favor, gentle sir,
Before you pass me by?—

"I've a load on my chest, and around my neck
A millstone swings,—Oh gee!
How many centuries must I wait
Till Gabriel blows for me?"
"That's easy, son, just watch me close,"
Said the Ghost of Napo-leon;
And the Ghost held its fingers up to the light.
And crooked them one by one.

"You speak in parables, kind sir!"
Said the King. "Can't you be more clear?
I'll give you the only thing I've got—
My pet—to name the year."

[xiv]

"You can take my Whifflebat," the Kaiser suggested.

"I'm not quite sure, so you'll have to ask
  Somebody else," said Nap;
"But you'll never get through those pearly gates,
  No matter how loud you rap!"

So saying, the gracious Ghost bowed low
And flitted away from there,
And the patriarch put a moss-covered crown
On the spot where he once had hair;
And the patriarch likewise laid himself
On his couch of dry verbena,
For the years are long and the sun is hot
On the sands of St. Helena!

HUMPTY-DUMPTY
WILLIAM & CO.

"Who's going to win this war?" demanded the Kaiser.

CHAPTER I

SOOTHSAYING COBBLER PREDICTS WAR

THE big war which has been occupying all Europe and parts of Asia began in the year 1914, but before we proceed further with events in chronology, let us hear from the Kaiser. We are enabled to present exclusively for the benefit of our many readers, thanks to our alert correspondent, a dialogue between that pompous official and his soothsaying cobbler which shows that the Kaiser was forewarned as well as forearmed. The prophecy was made in an anteroom of the Royal Palace.

"What is this I hear?" roared the Kaiser as he turned uneasily in his chair.

" 'Tis as I was saying, my lord,—we are going to have a considerable war," returned the Soothsaying Cobbler, assuming an humble-pie attitude.

"Don't trifle with me, cobbler; truth is what I am seeking!"

"I would risk my awl, my lord; you asked my veriest prophecy."

"Then tell me more; quick, tell me more!"

"The war will start in August, mayhap in the fourth week of July."

"Ya, ya; go on! How long will it last?"

"It will last many months; it may last many years."

"Who will win? That is the question!"

"Ah, my lord,—would that I could tell! I would have no need of cobbling any longer for a living."

"Then who will start it?"

"They will all start together."

"You mean there will be more than four?"

"Yes, my lord; maybe twice four, maybe thrice four."

"Himmel,—am I dreaming? Where's my man-servant?"

"Under the linden tree, fast asleep."

"I would have him pinch me to be sure I am not in a trance!"

"You are quite yourself, my lord."

"How did you come by all this knowledge? You are a worthless fellow—begone!"

"No, no, my lord; I pray thee, hear me through. I can tell by the moon, the stars, the fox fire, the royal beeswax."

"What about the moon? There's nothing wrong that I can see."

"In May it seldom has the double ring, my lord."

"And the stars?"

"They have not been so blazing since I have been toiling at the bench."

"And the fox fire?"

"It is a prancing will-o'-the-wisp. And the

royal beeswax is all melted and run together. Ah, ha, ha!''

"Cobbler, this levity in the Royal Palace is unseemly!"

"Pardon, my lord; wars are truly serious affairs."

"Is there more to tell?"

"Not now; more later, perhaps, my lord."

A short silence followed as the Kaiser lit another cigar and bit the end savagely, wrapping himself in deep thought as he did so. The silence was broken when the Kaiser jumped suddenly to his feet. The jangling of his metal bric-à-brac and the dull thud caused by his heavy boots hitting the floor reminded one of the sound from the drum-and-cymbals department of an orchestra in the grand finale of a newly-discovered masterpiece.

"That gives me an idea!" declared the Kaiser as he slapped his thigh. "I have a hunch that you are right about it, but don't you tell another soul, not even a half-soul!"

For several minutes the Kaiser paced the floor, his hands clasped behind him and his head bent forward. A bugle sounded outside and the Royal Guard fell in for a drill.

"Be off to your cobbling, my good man!" ordered the Kaiser as he shook himself out of his reverie. "Hold yourself in readiness, for I may need more prophecies. If anyone should inquire as you go out, say you have cobbled another pair of riding boots for the Kaiser."

CHAPTER II

LEADING UP TO WAR

THE two months' notice of war given the Kaiser by his faithful footwear artist was worth
a great deal to both. It enabled the Kaiser to put
a fine edge on his Preparedness program, and it
enabled the cobbler to realize almost overnight his
life-time dream of a captaincy in the Kaiser's per-
sonal bodyguard at a stupendously increased wage.

Boom! they were off, with the Kaiser leading by
a helmet spike. Half a dozen nations which had
been nurtured in different schools of thought and
expression now smote each other savagely, and
they were later joined by others hopeful of sharing
in the spoils at the final reckoning.

Before diving too far into the middle, however,
let us follow events somewhat as they happened.

For several months prior to the summer of 1914
American tourists who went to Europe to shake off
home environments and aggravate the tipping evil
reported that Europe's sword was all but un-
sheathed. The war spirit was in the air. Restless-
ness not only seized royalty, but also obsessed the
patient ditch-digger, who had worked vainly these
many years for a raise in salary and a weekly half-
holiday as well. All persons felt the impulse alike,

—the gent in the silk sox, the gent in the cotton sox and the gent who wore no sox at all except to prayer meeting on Wednesday nights.

This alien spirit found concrete expression when a Serbian bookworm cruelly molested some Austrian royalty in Serajevo, the tiny capital of Bosnia. The angry Austrians laid the blame at the door of Serbian political leaders as the hatchers of the entire plot. The aged Emperor was down with the lumbago that day, but spurred on by the unusual developments he bounced out of bed like a boy and backed a caustic note to King Peter, the worshipped ruler of the Serbians.

Since King Peter possessed a much smaller army (though no less brave), he retreated to the mountains before answering the note. Accounts differ, but one had it that King Peter was in such a hurry to get away that he wrapped a goatskin around him and fled on a mule toward Nish. The royal seal had been sunk in the Danube, the royal seal-skins packed away in moth-balls, and the royal palace left in the care of a faithful bellhop. This bellhop also had supervision over the wine-cellar, and he had been charged to suffer nobody to enter it in addition to himself. After cursing his luck King Peter wrote a reply, suggesting that the matter be talked over at The Hague, a place where peace discussions had raged before the war put the delegates hopelessly to rout.

King Peter was plainly playing for time, and when the aged Emperor realized this he ceased writing notes and called his wrought-up cabinet together. It was about this time that the accredited Serbian diplomat in the Austrian capital was devouring a huge Vienna sausage. He dropped the dog without waiting to finish or settle with the proprietor. This diplomat presently reached King Peter's side and told tales that made the king quake in his ancient boots and send for the royal hemlock with all the haste of the venerable Mr. Socrates.

King George, the President of France and Czar Nicholas prayed fervently for peace, keeping one eye open, and the Pope addressed so many peace notes to the quarreling hosts that he contracted writer's cramp and had to be hauled to a hospital. Berlin reported the Kaiser praying with a face as long as a Presbyterian deacon, but without getting down on his knees.

News of the impending calamity having reached the United States, the frantic peace prayers were repeated among the usual dissemblers; but in spite of all these plausible supplications, war could not be headed off.

Tension at some of the serious conferences was so keyed up that the blink of an eyelash was nearly enough to start hostilities. Great significance was attached to several highly unfortunate incidents. A French aviator, munching his noon-day meal in the clouds, accidentally dropped a dried herring in Alsace. The townspeople fled in a panic and German lookouts reported an attempt to blow up the

King Peter went in the direction of Nish.

railway station. Spies in Paris reported that a veteran of the last big war had redeemed his wooden leg at a pawnshop and was primed for whatever might come. French spies in Berlin told Paris how the Kaiser had spent a memorable night with his staff in a beer garden conference, in which the party had consumed four enormous kegs of beer, whereas their normal capacity was only two kegs of moderate size.

The Czar was seen dashing on horseback toward the German border, and King George was reliably reported to have called off a championship game of cricket with the Premier, an unheard-of thing for him to do. A party of Austrian barnstormers seized a Serbian fishing smack on the Danube, undoubtedly to take a harmless pleasure trip. This overt and high-handed act brought a loud protest from King Peter, whose anger was so great that his neck melted a celluloid collar a friend had kindly loaned him.

CHAPTER III

DECLARATIONS ARE EXCHANGED

KING GEORGE graciously offered the wine
room of Buckingham Palace for a sober, level-
headed conference, intending to turn on cool blasts
from his refrigerating plant in case any delegate
should wax too warm. The Kaiser and his clan
declined with thanks, anticipating that they might
also be expected to visit the Tower of London
after nightfall. The Germans held a meeting to
which King George was not invited reciprocally or
any other way. This was exclusively a side-arms-
and-helmets affair, and much business in a short
space of time is said to have been transacted. Left
out in the cold, King George flew to the side of the
President of France, and they also talked over vital
matters.

French and German peasants peeking across the
border to see what was the matter were manhan-
dled by the German border police and went home
to tell how grossly their countries had been in-
sulted. A Russian cavalryman dashed into an East
Prussian town to cop a farewell mug of beer, and
the burgomaster sent word to the Kaiser that the
Czar had made a start toward Berlin.

The hops of Bohemia were unusually thick that

A Belgian refugee en route to Holland.

year, but were no thicker than declarations of war for a time. The Kaiser ordered the Czar to quit massing so many black beards along the border, or serious trouble would follow. When the Czar summoned sixteen more armies, the Kaiser declared war. Executing a nimble right-about-face, the Kaiser flung a declaration at France. Great Britain, the child of unpreparedness among the European nations, surprised the Kaiser with a flat-footed declaration of war. The French minister announced a state of war with the Kaiser. Austria sent a defi to the Czar and little Montenegro stung Austria from behind.

Belgium piped a war refrain unto the Kaiser after that dignitary had written King Albert for permission to trample down his corn and subjects. King Albert told the Kaiser not to venture into his country on pain of being locked up; but the Kaiser paid no attention and came lumbering on, preceded by his mighty howitzers. King George hastened to assure King Albert that the English sympathized with the Belgians, and that if any help were needed, a handful of Irish policemen would be sent to make the Germans behave. King Albert finally hollered, but it was then too late, and his good subjects were forced to strap their beds on their backs and go to live with their Dutch cousins.

Japan, a restless, opportunist little nation which raises rice and tea and owns a crowded island not far from California, now shouted a megaphone declaration of war at the Kaiser. The crafty Japs first

Grave fears were felt for King Constantine.

seized the Kaiser's island possessions in the Pacific
Ocean. These were the Caroline Islands, than
which there are none more fertile. The Japs well-
nigh frightened the natives into hysterics, and then
waved the red flag at the little German band
cooped up in the garrison at Tsing-Tao, China, and
from that moment cut off the supply of good things
to eat.

The Kaiser swore to get even for this, and in
other ways he was not idle. He frantically wrote
and telegraphed his poor kinfolks in Europe to help
him realize his ambition. These kinfolks included
King Constantine of Greece, who by some accident
had married the Kaiser's sister, and who lay sick
abed with a supposedly fatal malady. This was
the first chance the King of Greece had ever had to
snub a well-to-do relative, and he was entirely un-
decided what to do. The common people wanted
him to stand by his Serb allies and fight the Kaiser,
but Mrs. Constantine begged her husband not to
harass her troubled brother. The King finally
took the advice of his wife against the counsel of
his premier, but he reserved the right to change his
mind with the changing fortunes of the Kaiser.
For weeks the King clung to the mortal coil, lying
just outside of death's door but never actually en-
tering it, much to the sorrow of the rank and file of
his wrought-up subjects.

Since swift retribution had failed to overtake
King Peter for his previous literary efforts, he now
made bold to send a caustic note to the Kaiser,

seeking to place the blame for the war, and punctuating his vital points with the crassest profanity.

"I wouldn't think of sending him my autograph," the angry Kaiser confided to his councillors. "Just lie low and we will catch the little rat and put him in the hoosegow."

So the Kaiser fitted out an expedition to nab King Peter at the royal palace, and ordered a messenger to bring back the glad tidings. The messenger returned to the Kaiser with a lot of good wines, but no Peter.

"I have the honor to bring you bad news," declared the messenger, hanging his head at the executioner's angle.

"What is that? Out with it!" shouted the Kaiser.

"King Peter gave us the slip!"

"Damn it!" ejaculated the Kaiser. "I could take a butterfly net and catch him myself!"

CHAPTER IV

WHEREIN THE SWISS RISE UP

"NOT one cent for offense, but thousands for defense!"

This ringing slogan and shibboleth was sounded by the brave Swiss people as soon as the first war cloud had floated over the historic Jungfrau, and time has justified its wisdom. No sooner were the model dairies and chocolate factories of Switzerland put in jeopardy than the wise old heads of the cabinet sent an ultimatum to the Kaiser and the world that trespassing would be opposed by 500,-000 irate citizens crouching behind death-dealing instruments. This was ten times as many loyal troopers as could have been raised in sixty days in political America. Here was Preparedness raised to the nth power, a lesson to the civilized world and a marvel to the uncivilized.

The Kaiser had so many responsibilities already that he decided not to knock the large chip off the small Swiss shoulder, and all the other belligerent nations arrived at the same conclusion. Switzerland is probably the smallest nation in the world, and likewise the most respected. The Swiss navy also gave an excellent account of itself, maintaining

A war-time diversion in Sunny Italy.

a vaunted supremacy over Lake Lucerne, even to the point of keeping out the Kaiser's slippery submarines.

Little time was lost by the other small countries in barring the door against the various invaders. Portugal agreed to lend the services of her gunboat provided England would keep all comers out of her back yard. She also gave up her ancient mariners and fish officials as an aid to Allied navigation.

Holland, farther north, was early thrown into a stew of excitement. This is a scraggly, well-watered country whose coast line as shown in the maps resembles the jagged edge of a rip-saw. It is bounded on the east by Germany and on the west by the North Sea, and has naturally been unable to expand in either direction. But it is a warmer country than three years ago by reason of close proximity to the European holocaust.

While the Dutch layman was suspicious of the Kaiser's game, the King was another of the Kaiser's poor relations and trusted the great ruler implicitly. For many years they had swapped Christmas presents, and in return the Kaiser had promised the great Dutchman to notify him in case of approaching war. The Dutch King was conservative and had never installed a telephone system, so the Kaiser sent Fritz, the royal aviator, with a warning note. Fritz was a college graduate and an exceedingly high-flying young man, and when he approached the Dutch palace he was flying so high that the winds prevented him from landing.

Fritz mistook the royal gardener for the King and dropped the note, which fell just outside the palace wall and was picked up by a baker. The baker could not make it out and handed it to a butcher, who could not make it out and handed it to a wax magnate, who recognized the Kaiser's signature and turned it over to the burgomaster, who summoned the royal footman and rushed it madly to the King.

The King turned several fast colors and shouted: "Take the royal rats and ferrets from the royal malt and let them gnaw the royal dikes! The enemy is coming and we must make the kingdom safe all around!"

The little animals did their duty and in a few hours Holland looked like a Swiss cheese submarine at high tide.

In traveling home from Holland, Fritz flew over Denmark. Sad story, mates! He threw overboard some ballast in the shape of a sandbag, and this simple fact explains why the Danes do not love the Kaiser any more. By a sad coincidence, Eric Stefansson was grubbing artichokes in a garden down below. Eric was one of Denmark's leading men of science, having once discovered a barber's pole at the northernmost point in Scandinavia. He had also smashed many an old Martin Frobisher and Sir Francis Drake record among the icebergs of the frigid north, and was the fit and proper person to decorate in the name of the King all rival explorers captured thereabout; and in that capacity

The ancient explorer had things coming his way.

had even hung a sunflower wreath around the goosle of old Dr. Cook.

Most of which was set forth elaborately on Eric's headstone, but even that could not bring him back. It is also proper to say in this connection that Eric was 102 years old and had never seen a "movie."

CHAPTER V

THE IRISH GO TO WAR

SINCE it was not a great step from the Home Rule fight to the war, the Irish enlisted liberally to help out their English brothers, although many held back to meet the next move by Parliament. The Irish Home Guard was a necessary precaution, because if all the men had gone to the front there is no telling what kind of government they would have had on returning to Erin's potato hills.

Hundreds volunteered to save the Belgians, since that kind of work always appeals to an Irishman. Although the English landed the Irish too late to hurl the Kaiser out of Belgium, in other ways the Irish were of tremendous assistance. To them is due the credit of saving the citizens— including the women, children, weak old men, parrots, canary birds and goats—in a disorderly retreat toward the interior, for who else was there to carry mattresses, family clocks, spinning wheels, trunks and bric-à-brac out of harm's way? None but the Irish! Didn't McGillicuddy lug a poor widow woman's soap premium organ all the way from Amsterdam to Brussels? And then, begorra, she had disappeared in the crowd!

A conservative hero—Tommy Atkins.

Another thing the Irish must get credit for when a fuller history of the war than this is written. They taught the Belgians what to do when out of ammunition—to hand the Germans bricks from demolished buildings. In the old country they call it throwing Irish confetti, and this method of winning an argument seldom fails. Ask Charlie Kelly.

The world has the Irish to thank for all the advancement of a century in free masonry, brick masonry, public guardianship, bartending and the Mulligan Stew. In spite of the fact that the English at the beginning of the war told the Irishmen they were worth their weight in gold, many packed up their goods and chattels and sailed for America, and on reaching this land of liberty joined the New York police force and are making useful citizens.

CHAPTER VI

IMPORTANT MEETING OF ALLIED LEADERS

A HIGHLY important meeting of Allied leaders was held in London at this juncture for the purpose of bringing the war to a sudden end. King George sent out notices asking the other crowned heads to come into the convention with a definite plan. He opened the meeting with the following well-chosen words:

"If it please your graces, we are gathered here to-day to discuss how best to rid ourselves of a considerable obsession."

This veiled reference to the Kaiser was greeted with an outburst of hand-claps.

"I think we understand each other. This Nemesis of the peace-loving citizenship of the eastern hemisphere must certainly be eradicated."

"Right!" shouted the other rulers in chorus.

"My good people are fixed in their resolve to compromise nothing until their national ideals have been fully realized. The determination of our allies must be no less strong."

"We are with you!" yelled the President of France. "Just lead the way."

"It is well known that the Kaiser wishes to con-

The kings discussed the Kaiser's fate.

quer the world. We must place ourselves squarely on record. Do I hear a motion to that effect?''

"Your presiding lordship, I make such a motion,'' said the Czar, winking at King Peter of Serbia. "William was an old college chum of mine, but fate has always decreed that he should be a Humpty-Dumpty.''

"I second the motion,'' said King Peter.

"Your presiding lordship,'' began the King of Italy, "I should like to discuss that motion.''

"The King of Italy is out of order,—the vote always precedes the discussion, and unless there is objection I will declare the motion passed. We will now discuss ways and means of attaining the end so much desired by all.''

"Your presiding lordship,'' began the Czar, "the weakest spot in the Kaiser's line is through Serbia. I favor driving up the Danube as the quickest way to end the war.''

"May I interrupt?'' asked King Peter. "I think the Czar is mistaken. The most important point to begin a drive is at the Pea-vine Hay Farm in Flanders.''

"That cannot be,'' returned King George, "because my men say it is impossible to break through. Are there any more suggestions?''

"It seems to me that a feint along the Alsatian frontier would cause the Kaiser to weaken his lines in northern France,'' said the President of the French.

"Are there many Germans in Alsace?'' inquired

the Czar. "I mean are there as many per square mile as there are in Poland, for instance?"

"That would be hard to say, but we could send some South Africans to find out."

"I have a plan," chirped the King of Montenegro, who up to this time had been lying low. "Every morning at ten o'clock, I am reliably informed, the Kaiser goes into the royal garden to inspect the gooseberry bushes. Why not send an aviator to drop something on him?"

"I should not like to be that aviator," said the Czar, "unless I had a pretty large insurance policy and wanted excitement worse than I do."

"Now you are talking," ventured King Peter.

The King of Belgium arose to his feet. "I don't understand the purpose of the meeting," he announced. "I have been sitting here half an hour in the hope that somebody would enlighten me. This body makes me think of a Brooklyn board of trade."

"King Albert must be informed," interposed King George. "We are here to discuss how to get rid of the Kaiser in as painless a way as possible."

"Yes, but I don't see what life insurance has got to do with it," persisted the Belgian king. "If somebody would suggest tunneling to Berlin and putting a giant cracker under the Kaiser, that would interest me. Likewise, I should like to know how long this war is going to last and who is going to win it. After that I will go and water my horse."

"If my jolly jester were here I would call on him to answer," said King George, with a twinkle in his eye; "but in his absence, maybe somebody will volunteer."

King George looked hard at the Czar, who now made bold to say:

"Do you think I would tell this bunch if I knew? I would place a side bet and win a barrel of money!"

CHAPTER VII

ACROSS THE BROAD ATLANTIC

LET us now leave Europe for a time, gentle reader, and view the scene across the broad Atlantic, where the war news had caused tremendous excitement, especially among the powder magnates and other things that blow up, including a well known political party. The powder magnates gave promise of taking rank in America's new crop of millionaires, and the politicians wondered what the war would shake down to them, if anything.

The scene is Washington, where the President had rung for his nimble Secretary of State.

"Good morning, Mr. Secretary," was the way the President started off the conversation.

"Mornin'," returned the Secretary.

"Take that rocker,—it is more comfortable."

"Thanks, awfully."

"You are not quite yourself, I fear, Mr. Secretary. Won't you have something to drink? Something soft, I mean?"

"No, I thank you; I just got one as I passed the corner drug store."

"How about a cigar?"

How to stop the big war was the question.

"Nothing at all, thank you; I do not dissipate any more. I believe you asked me to come over to see about getting peace."

"Yes, I have written a note to the Kaiser which I think fittingly expresses our regret over the chaotic conditions. Will you be good enough to sign it?"

"I would rather not sign before reading the note."

"Of course not; I didn't mean that."

"Things look very serious in Europe and Mexico. You remember I said I hoped there would be no kind of war while I was secretary."

"You said it all right."

"Well, I am still hoping that way."

"I don't quite understand you."

"Mexico seems determined to fight with us."

"I think I have a way to handle them."

"I trust so, because something in my bones tells me we are going to be drawn in."

"Ahem! Let us hope for the best."

"Anything is possible, at home or abroad, and I was wondering what would become of the deserving Democrats."

"You needn't worry about that. Are you ready to sign the note?"

"Yes, there's my fist. I favor peace at any price for everybody. If the nations would only live up to the peace treaties I drafted the world would be a much better place to live in."

"There can be no doubt of it. Would you mind

signing this note to Mexico? The note says if the Mexicans don't quit pestering our citizens we shall look with grave concern upon the situation."

"I suggest that we strike out the word 'grave.' "

"What's the matter with it?"

"The word carries a very unfortunate suggestion."

"I did not mean it that way."

(Enter the Secretary of the Navy.)

"Take a seat, Mr. Secretary; how are things down in Raleigh?" asked the President.

"Fine as split silk," returned the Secretary, right off the bat.

"We were just talking about some little affairs of state. What can I do for you?"

"I came to report a secret campaign to enlarge the American navy. They say the prospect of a big war in Europe calls for more ships over here. I can't see it."

"Whom do you mean by 'they'?"

"I don't know who they are, but they are mighty busy."

"Suppose you find out whatever you can about it."

"Yes, sir."

"By the way, when you go out, I wish you would mail these letters. They are important."

"All right, sir."

Two weather-beaten admirals who asked that their names be withheld were waiting in an anteroom as the Secretary of the Navy filed by.

"What do you think of him?" asked Admiral No. 1.

"He belongs on a Mississippi River tugboat," replied Admiral No. 2.

"I'll bet fifty dollars to a burnt ginger cake he don't know this minute where the Pacific Fleet is located!"

"I'll make another bet he don't know where the Pacific Ocean is located!"

"Do you suppose he will ever resign?"

"There is not the slightest hope."

CHAPTER VIII

BACK TO SEETHING EUROPE

WE shall now retrace our footsteps to Europe, which was not quite the safest place in the world to be, but by far the most interesting.

The Czar had thrown countless Russian peasants through the forbidding Carpathian Mountains, instructing them to muzzle dangerous Austrians and bring as many to Siberia as possible. The brave, excitable French were overflowing into their old territories, Alsace and Lorraine, and they swore they would not return until French was again taught in the public schools. The British were getting ready and would soon arrive at the front, word from London said.

In the meanwhile, the versatile Kaiser had flung his fighting men in every conceivable direction, and finally had deployed several small armies in the air and underground. He reached a tentacle toward the coast towns Dunkirk and Calais, which are uncomfortably close to London. In return, King George hurled bitter anathemas at him, and called loudly for reinforcements in the direction of the cricket fields.

The hapless Belgians were spending wakeful nights. They no longer slept with trinkets under

Von Kluck turned the goose-step toward Paree.

their pillows, peacefully dreaming of rescue parties and a thoroughly redeemed countryside. They burned more bridges behind them, lugged their duds out of the great cities and swore to get even for the inconvenience if it took them a thousand years.

After having cleared Belgium of all antagonistic elements, seized the treasury and the commissary, shot peep-holes through the cathedral spires and reduced old castles to hopeless junk, von Kluck, the Kaiser's right-hand man in the early stages, hit a bee-line for the gay lights of Paris. He announced German Night in the French capital, and urged every soldier to do his level best to be there on time. The Kaiser's goose-step was carrying him far. Goose-step is simply another word for co-operation, without which nobody can get anywhere.

The Allied outposts were swept back before they could gain a toe-hold to halt von Kluck's onward march, and it appeared that the Germans would feast in Paris restaurants that night in spite of all that could be done. Their army was literally a mailed football team, primed from head to hoof for a pushing, shoving, claw-hammer attack. Could it keep from fumbling the ball, it would certainly reach the goal, and all would be over except the alarums within.

In the French army, however, existed a prodigy named Joffre. His first name matters not, and in addition, is unknown to us. General Joffre was prodigious enough to be a first-class genius, as events amply proved. He had not played tackle on his college team for nothing, and consequently knew perfectly how to stop a tandem formation and plant it prone on Mother Earth. He organized a flying wedge that deflected the von Kluck tandem and finally threw it back into a large river. Some of the Germans landed right side up, some upside down, and still others floated with the current and have not communicated with their families since. Many got an all-over bath for the first time since leaving home.

The Kaiser watched the battle from a plum thicket and when he saw General Joffre's insurmountable barrier he ordered the noble commander to describe an arc to side-step the lunging Frenchmen. But the French gladiators described a corresponding arc which spoiled the first-named arc entirely; and von Kluck retired sullenly to high ground and announced that German Night in Paris had been postponed indefinitely.

Von Kluck's star rose quickly and set in the same manner. His name never finds its way into the newspaper headlines any more, which gives considerable point to the suggestion that he has joined the Uhlans, the Dinosauruses and other objects that are now hopelessly extinct.

General Joffre, on the other hand, has played in better luck. Having taken the part of a male modern Joan of Arc in France's great dilemma, he has more than held his own. In many subsequent encounters he has been called upon, and no untoward circumstance has ever arisen to mar his brilliant career. Unlike most weighty personages who go to their final reward unappreciated by their fellowmen, General Joffre is the subject of much hero worship in the living present. He is an easy winner in all popularity contests and has had hundreds of babies named after him, and eventually his name will appear on war implements, talcum powder, hair tonic, French perfume and cigars.

CHAPTER IX

THE ALLIES SIGN A PACT

SIR EDWARD GREY has convinced suave diplomats everywhere that he has a longer head than most of them. He has been awarded the red suspenders as the smoothest gent in all the world, and if he should ever use his talent in the promotion of mines and railroads he would soon be exceedingly well off.

Anticipating that the Czar might be embarrassed by a powder shortage and conclude a separate peace, that France might be forced to bow to the will of the Kaiser, and that the question of supremacy would lie between the British navy and the Kaiser's army, Sir Edward called representatives of the leading Allies together at Paris. He pointed out with incontrovertible logic the manifold advantages for all to fight to a fist-and-skull finish.

"If Russia should not fight," declared Sir Edward as he hit his left palm a staggering blow with his right fist, "France would be terribly embarrassed. If France should not fight, Russia would be sorely pressed. You can easily see how each could get nowhere."

"By the same reasoning," chirped the French diplomat, "England would soon be in a devil of a

The diplomats hastened to sign the articles.

fix. The Kaiser would hitch his horses in West-minster Abbey and turn Buckingham Palace into a grog shop!''

"Now you have reached the milk in the cocoa-nut," agreed the Russian envoy, Skiovitch, as he stroked his massive beard with smug satisfaction.

The advantages were so obvious that the trio nearly fought for the privilege of signing first. Sir Edward actually upset the ink, thus putting the articles in serious danger, while the French envoy poked his elbow in the eye of Skiovitch. Once all the papers were signed, they were stuck together with the royal glue, and Sir Edward handed each diplomat a copy and each went on his way re-joicing.

On account of the bottled-up nature of the east-ern hemisphere, Skiovitch was forced to travel half-way around the world to reach the side of the anxious Czar. By disguising himself successively as a Tyrolean yodler, a South American coloniza-tion agent and a dissembling old monk, he finally reached home.

"Did you have a pleasant journey?" inquired the Czar with undisguised cordiality.

"Equally pleasant and profitable," returned Skiovitch gleefully.

"Bully!" cried the Czar. "Have three fingers of this health restorer! And you succeeded in tying the hands of the French and the British so they couldn't leave us with the bag to hold?"

"Absolutely; we have nothing to fear."

"Let me take a look at those articles."

Skiovitch reached his hand into his inside pocket. The agreement was not there. He tried his hip pocket. It was not there, either. He searched the lining of his coat, but without success. Then he started beating his hip, his thigh and his chest until there was danger that he would beat himself to death.

"I must have left the articles in my monk's costume down in Turkey!" announced the envoy as the awful truth dawned upon him.

"Bonehead,—we are ruint! Run quick and put a want ad. in all the papers!" shrieked the unhappy Czar.

CHAPTER X

THE FINANCIAL SHOE PINCHES

AFTER a season of continuous racket the financial shoe began to pinch the nations at war. The Kaiser borrowed from his subjects and the Allies asked Mr. Morgan to touch the American people for a cool billion in gold. Not since European titles had been peddled around had there been such a heavy demand for money from this side. A committee of polite bankers came to the United States and got half of the amount requested, and they vowed the money would be spent here for things needed to cut the Kaiser's career short. Munitions makers favored the loan strongly, but doubting Thomases declared it would be a cold day before the common people got their savings back. No less an authority than Rudyard Kipling wrote that England might declare a moratorium at the end of hostilities, provided hostilities should ever end. Mr. Kipling gets a dollar a word for his writings, so he ought to know what he is talking about.

Since the Allies were spending fifty millions daily, their pressing need of loan funds must be apparent. Where the money is coming from nobody appears to know, but the war is a very ex-

A committee of polite bankers requested a loan.

pensive pastime, and some doubt has been expressed that all of the fighting countries are worth as much as they have burnt up and torn down.

Europeans are popularly supposed to have made investments in America totaling a billion dollars, and it has been the hope for many years that these securities could be brought back home. It looks as if the munitions makers are the only people in a position to do this. The subject of money is a very wide and deep one. Money is very much like the fourth dimension and womankind—elusive until you've cornered them and puzzling thereafter.

Having never dealt in more than three figures, we shall leave the solution to Wall Street. It does not require a brain bigger than an English walnut, however, to offer a cure for every financial ill in Europe. Let the warring nations form a giant trust to exploit war movies. The American movie fans will not only pay all war debts, but will furnish a surplus whereby each down-at-the-heel nation can again hunch its way to a respectable place among the élite of this terrestrial ball.

CHAPTER XI

THE KAISER NAILS FALSEHOODS

"HO, ho, har, har, hee, hee, wow!!!!"
Our faithful correspondent at the front looked up suddenly from a bowl of concentrated pea-soup and observed an individual writhing in paroxysms of laughter.

"Whoopee, har, har, har!!!"

"Raus mit Ihm!" snarled our alert correspondent in his best German as he tried to balance several peas on his knife. Then, indicating a sad scene outside, our special leg man at the front cautioned the intruder:

"Can't you see you'll be waking somebody from a nap, you noisy fellow?"

The individual put on a serious face at once, poking his sea-foam bosom out eleven inches as he did so. Then he glared mercilessly at our well-paid scribe and ordered:

"Mind your own business, you meddlesome knave! I would laugh in the face of Old Scratch if I wanted to!"

Nobody but the Kaiser could give vent to such a bold expression, and our correspondent now recognized him and wondered how they could have been thrown together so unceremoniously.

"Just light out from here if you don't like the

The Kaiser laughed until his ribs rattled.

bill of fare," continued the Kaiser, pressing an evident advantage. "Don't get on your ear or you might be called at sunrise, as long as I'm running this joint!"

"I beg your pardon, most perfect gentle knight," returned our now thoroughly humble correspondent, happily recalling a passage from the Chaucer of his early college days. "I didn't think it was you because I never heard of your laughing that way before."

"Never laughed, indeed! What lying authors have you been reading after?"

"Shaw, Kipling, Irvin S. Cobb and Paul Rockwell."

"Rockwell—Rockwell? Yes, he hails from Atlanta. That place gets into everything. But you had better read some Don Marquis fiction, a poem by Arthur Guiterman or Fuzzy Woodruff's incomparable sporting page. To be up on the war you should read William Bayard Hale and Major Moraht."

"I have read after all of them and also Appius Claudius Nealy. How about Hilaire Belloc?"

"There is no such person! Here is a London paper I managed to get which says I am crying these days because I can see my finish. They say I am digging ditches and working in the harvest. That's what makes me laugh. I nearly keel over!"

"Your story interests me."

"Listen, young man, and when you go back home, tell them the truth. I laugh quite frequently,

One of the Kaiser's body-guard.

just like anybody else with a sense of humor. To-day I could not restrain myself. The writers who have never seen me say I am getting bald, nervous, infirm of step, restless, irritable, can't sleep o' nights. Don't you believe a word of it! I can still make it around without a crutch. I can kick higher than your head! It would amaze you how quickly I can travel from one front to the other. Does not that give the lie to my accusers? As for my armies, they are everywhere supreme. They will still be around here when most of the others have gone to a place we don't like to think about.

"Just listen to this sample: 'The Kaiser has addressed an appeal to his panic-stricken people to hold out until the last potato skin is gone. He says, "Will my self-sacrificing people fail to back up the army's triumphs? The writer does not believe it." '

"Young man, that is an unadulterated fake. I never referred to myself as a writer. It beats the Dutch!"

"I believe you."

"Just give these cartoons the once-over. Your Mr. Darling has me sweating violently at Arras. I have never even perspired there. I have let the French sweat. Your Mr. Carter puts furrows in my brow and gives me a hideous mutton suet mustache. The ends of my mustache turn upward, as you can see for yourself. Nelse Harding, of your 'Brooklyn Eagle,' makes me look foolish. Ach, it is to laugh!"

"I don't blame you for laughing, but as for crying, I have read your past, and, taken with what I know of your present, I am convinced that you haven't cried since you were a baby!"

"Har, har, har!!! that's a good one, young man! Did you say your name was Lawrence?"

"No, Dave pompadours his hair. He is in Washington helping the Democrats to hold on."

"Well, I'm glad to meet you, anyway; and when you return home you must set me right. Present my compliments to the Mayor of Baltimore for his generous reception of Captain Koenig, our brave submarine commander."

"Will you send any message to King George as I pass through London?"

"Young man, I will see him in hell first!"

CHAPTER XII

ITALY'S GUM-SHOE CAMPAIGN

SOUTH of the Alps lies Italy, an unassuming nation which for many years was cuffed around Europe, but which of late has taken a decided brace. Italy is shaped like a boot, and she entered the war to get a boot-strap from Austria, which would include the provinces of Trent and Trieste.

Italy excels in opera singers, light wines, spaghetti magnates, organ grinders, trained monkeys, gondola romances and condensed goat's milk, and she was the first country to demonstrate that treaties are mere scraps of paper. Germany, Austria and Italy were tied together as Allies by a long-standing agreement. They not only traded with each other, but would fight for each other if the occasion ever arose. That was before Germany and Austria got into the hornets' nest with the Allies. So at the first opportunity Italy gum-shoed her way into the conflict and began to give her former bed-fellows something to do in the extreme South.

The fighting in this theater was nearly all above the clouds, which called for sure-footed mountain climbers with unusually stable equilibrium. To

Corporal Caruso was very proud of his job.

make things easier for his soldiers the good King of Italy dug roads through the snowy cliffs, winding them like the boulevards that belt real estate subdivisions in countries still at peace; but there were many places which only an Angora goat or a Ford automobile could climb. Peasant yodlers who were temporarily out of jobs in grand opera were greatly in demand to call the troops into traps. These yodlers were so successful that they soon carried all the medals, chevrons and epaulets that they could stand up under.

At death grips so high in the sky, the opposing hosts presented a very spectacular appearance. They offered every element needed in the twentieth-century movie production except frantic love affairs and a cross-country chase after a pet goose. Many of these soldiers were higher than they had ever been before, or would ever be, so they pinned their faith on St. Peter and the Kaiser, respectively.

Our own Amato, Scotti and Caruso have not been subjected to these awful dangers, but are industriously blowing holes in spaghetti. Caruso likes it better than the monkey-house. He has risen to a corporalcy and is so proud that he has popped all the buttons off his vest.

CHAPTER XIII

GRAVEDIGGERS THREATEN STRIKE

THE British army on the west front faced a serious crisis when the Ancient and Rancid Order of Concatenated Gravediggers demanded a twelve-hour day and appropriate pay for the work done. The men pointed out that in the unenlightened days of the Crusades eighteen hours was required, but that times had changed and half of twenty-four hours was all that any man should work, even in so noble a cause. They also set forth that less work and more pay everywhere has the Sanction of Society, which ought to be a-plenty.

Peace was assured in a compromise which held it to be unlawful for any gravedigger to officiate at more than twenty-four interments per day, whereas the average had been thirty-six.

Two former citizens of the United States who had drifted into the army started the reform movement in a casual conversation.

"How long you been diggin' graves, mate?" asked Gravedigger No. 1 during a pause in the tumult.

"Nigh onto forty years," replied Gravedigger No. 2. "Why do you ask?"

"For information. I was wonderin' if it wasn't

time for a man to take a vacation after he had dug
graves that long.''

"I never have time to take a vacation. So many
folks have to be 'tended to, you know.''

"But don't you never get tired bendin' yo' back?
I was thinkin' o' this war business—it is turrible.''

"You are right,—I never saw nothin' like it.''

"Why, man, I can't snatch a wink o' sleep before somebody yells, 'Bring your shovel over
here!' ''

"Now you are talkin'.''

"It does look like they wouldn't work a man to
death and give him nothin' to speak of to support
a large family.''

"You are exactly right.''

"I haven't had my foot out of the grave, it
seems, in two weeks. What do you think about
takin' the matter up at the next meetin'?''

"I favor it.''

"Better strike than be rooked out o' all our
time.''

"You bet your life.''

"By the way, I see where Congress has give
the railroad men a raise.''

"Yep, they was a long time comin' to it.''

"Them capitalists will never feel the difference.''

"Naw, they got money no man can count.''

"I tell you what Congress ought to do next—''

"What?''

"Raise the newspaper men.''

"This war business is turrible," said
Gravedigger No. 1.

"How so?"

"Well, it ain't nuthin' to me, but I got a friend what works on a small-town newspaper—it's in Dothan, Ala.—an' ain't had a raise in forty years."

"What do you think o' that!"

"He's an old re-write man, works twelve hours regular in a country shop an' ain't even got no show to draw a pension."

"I feel sorry for that guy."

"I believe in everybody gettin' plenty; the farmer too—poor devil!"

"So do I. I got a friend with a family o' six what works twelve hours a day at a grocery for thirty-five dollars a month."

"The government ought to look into that."

"But he never gets sick—can't afford to—and the boss calls him his right-hand man."

"Did you hear about King George?"

"What about him?"

"He's offered a big reward for the Kaiser."

"You don't say so!"

"I got a scheme to catch that gink."

"I wouldn't turn him over to King George."

"What would you do?"

"Put the Kaiser in a cage and haul him around the United States! There's millions in it, man!"

CHAPTER XIV

TURKEY MARKED FOR A CARVING

ALTHOUGH the Sultan of Turkey married a great many wives, in other respects he was no fool. In order to carry out his devilment undisturbed in the slums of Asia he made his vast empire secure with two padlocks—the Gallipoli Peninsula, a piece of land shaped like a strip of bacon southwest of Constantinople, and the Bosporus, the eastern gateway into the Black Sea, the Czar's private inland waterway.

Investigation by a British army commander in the Far Southeast revealed that while everybody was busy in Europe, the Sultan was whetting his knife on the poor Armenians. Religious differences caused the Sultan to attempt the extermination of a million of these people, and but for the timely arrival of the British and the Russians he would soon have accomplished his nefarious purpose. Two hundred thousand were saved, and consequently were not hung up to bleach on the Sultan's locust trees.

As soon as King George and the Czar caught the Sultan in this pastime, they vowed they would give Turkey a carving. The Turks were to be thrown bodily out of Europe and their two padlocks taken

The Turks whetted their knives on
the poor Armenians.

forever away from them. The Czar wanted a trade route opened through the great bodies of water to the southeast of his realm, and King George was also suspected of wanting several heavily fortified points to match Gibraltar. If the Czar could only get more seaports, just one nation would surpass Russia in population, resources and mental acumen, and that would be China. Hence it appeared that King George and the Czar might have a healthy scrap when time came to divide up the spoils.

The Sultan suddenly countermanded an order for British sardines which he had planned to provide for his populous family, and this was taken by the Allies as equivalent to a declaration of war. Before they could hand him a formal note he had tied to the Kaiser and flung defis at every nation for miles around.

The Sultan explained his precipitate action as follows:

"Whenever a man runs to get a pistol to shoot me, I always overtake him with a sandbag."

CHAPTER XV

VON TIRPITZ PAYS HIS RESPECTS

ONE crisp morning at sun-up an old man with a Joseph Smith beard hobbled to the front door of the Royal Palace and asked for the Kaiser. To Americans interned in Berlin he suggested Benjamin Franklin of bread-line days, for he carried a long loaf of sandwich bread under his arm.

"I want to see the Kaiser," said the visitor to the royal bellhop.

"Who wishes to see him?" demanded the royal bellhop, assuming the forbidding air of a J. P. Morgan office-boy.

"Von Tirpitz," said the old sea-dog, for 'twas none other than he.

"Von Spigots, did you say?"

"No, von Tirpitz."

"Have you got a card, Mr. von Tippetts?"

"No, don't trifle with me, boy; tell the Kaiser von Tirpitz says to please show his nose."

The flunkey disappeared and in a few moments the Kaiser came running to the front.

"Good morning, Admiral—come in," said the Kaiser. "I have a new bellhop. I hope he got your name."

"Won't you have a beer on me?" asked the Kaiser.

"Well, he got mixed up a little. I haven't had a visiting card since I was in London."

"What can I do for you—lend you any money?"

"Oh, no, I can't spend what I have. I want a submarine a week if you would win this war."

"Tell them I said to let you have it. Of course we must win."

At this point in the dialogue the Kaiser noticed that von Tirpitz had brought his breakfast with him.

"Why do you bring bread into the Royal Palace?" he demanded. "Do you think this is a free-soup joint?"

"Don't you worry," shot back the old salt. "I have no regular boarding place, so I carry my meals along. It is much more satisfactory."

"I see; sometimes I feel like eating in the street myself. I hate to be so formal."

"I never am."

"Won't you have a beer on me? You look awfully dry."

"I don't care if I do. This baker's loaf sticks in my throat."

"Ach! Gut Heil!"

"Here's looking at you!"

A messenger brought in a note.

"It is of no consequence," announced the Kaiser. "Only a despatch saying von Hindenburg has captured 200,000 more Russian bread-baskets."

"Those Russians can eat more and do less work than any people I know."

"There is only one remedy."

"What is that?"

"Deal with them on the spot."

Another messenger entered.

"A note from Wilson saying he is getting real angry over our submarine campaign," said the Kaiser, with a yawn.

"I would pay no attention to such impudence!" shouted von Tirpitz as he banged his fist down on the table.

"Just kick that waste-basket over this way," was the Kaiser's significant reply.

CHAPTER XVI

SIR IAN'S THRILLING ADVENTURE

ALTHOUGH the English vowed they had no designs on the Turks' main city in Europe, they refrained from putting their sentiments in writing with the Czar. King George hastened to tell the Czar not to send any troops to drive the hapless Turks off the Gallipoli Peninsula. A letter which has fallen into our hands is the best evidence:

"Nicholas, Czar of all the Russias,
    "Petrograd.
"Dear Friend Nick:
    "I wish you would not send any of your armies down to Gallipoli until I call for them. I have a young general who thrives best in a hot climate and I want to give him a real try-out. He answers to the name of Sir Ian. We shall soon whip them to a hopeless frazzle. Come to see me when you can.

                    "Yours fraternally,
                                        "George."

Sir Ian started for Gallipoli a comparatively young man, in splendid health and spirits, recking little what was coming to him. The great Allied fleets went ahead to pave the way, with more ammunition than discretion, as events amply proved. The ships belched sheets of flame toward the sequestered Turks and kicked up pluperfect chaos along the coast. The retreat of a handful of Turks caused the British Admiralty to announce an important victory, and to predict that in two weeks the fleet would force its way through to Constantinople and rout the Sultan from his favorite retreat.

For many years the Turks had been preparing for just such eventualities. Although several outer forts had been smashed beyond recognition, dozens of other strongholds bristled with guns like the back of a porcupine at bay. Turkish valor was directed by German gumption, and many of the King's medal winners bit the sandy promontories, never to rise again.

After several futile sorties and failing to get Irish hod-carrier reinforcements he had requested, Sir Ian answered a call home. Sir Ian's present address is unknown. One report says he is a brevet major somewhere in France; another, that he is somewhere in England, all dressed up in a uniform and with no place to go.

CHAPTER XVII

ADMIRAL LOSES FLAGSHIP AND SELF

EVER since the famous Invisible Spanish Armada was sent to the bottom of the sea it has been the policy of the English navy to attack hostile fleets on sight, no matter how fast, how large, or how many. Well and good, but a certain reckless admiral once upon a time, through no fault of his own, had inferior ships. Sailing leisurely in the Pacific, expecting to encounter nothing more than a harmless Swede's catboat, the admiral butted into German sea rovers which had disregarded the British order to stay in the home ports.

The brave admiral fired the first shot, but he did not fire the last. His shells fell far short of the mark. For all we know, his powder was damp or had sea salt in it. At any rate, the Kaiser's gallant tars arched their shells into the skies and punctured the admiral's decks, and the straight-line shots made scrap-iron out of his spick-and-span turrets. Utterly unable to reciprocate, the admiral went down beneath the wave and thus plowed his way into history evermore. Some said he ran below and began pumping out the ocean; others that he climbed high into the rigging and yelled for assistance. All who saw him give up the ghost, however, testified to his perfect abandon.

The Admiral sank down beneath the wave.

When war was declared, many of the Kaiser's vessels were caught out of port, and they immediately began adding as much as possible to the general confusion. These ships slipped up on numerous banana schooners, removed the bananas and the best story-teller in the crew and sank the vessel without further ado. The Emden was a cruiser which wrought the most havoc and became known as the Scourge of the Sea. After many weeks of exciting adventures and close escapes she was sent to a coral resting-place.

Several amphibious members of the crew clung to a bed of sea-weed and floated to a cocoanut island, where they persuaded a family of monkeys to chuck down sufficient cocoanuts to avert hunger pangs and anything worse. Then they built a raft of bamboo and set sail for the mainland. The raft capsized and the tars were swallowed by a hungry whale, but were cast up Jonah fashion when the skipper smoked his pipe. They landed this time on a larger island, seized all the fiddler crabs and cove oysters, established a canning factory and are enjoying life and a prosperous trade with the natives for miles around.

CHAPTER XVIII

COLD WORK IS ENCOUNTERED

UNDERTAKERS who gave an unprecedented rush of business as an excuse for failing to go to war were fully justified in due time. The demand was so heavy that the old price of fifty-six dollars for an automobile hearse and twenty-five other obsequious items was reduced nearly seventy per cent. Had the bottom not dropped out of prices, the people would have insisted on government ownership in small towns.

Darwin's theory was gaining every day, since so many links were missing in boasted genealogical chains. Blue-book investigators had all they could do at a hundred dollars a link. Another seeming paradox was the sudden departure for the front of noble scions, while the fungus growth of great families remained at home to look after the women and children. The splendid specimens were mowed down and the weak did their best to revamp the race, but succeeded feebly.

Still, a great many giants will survive this war, and the average of their opsonic index will be so high that American athletes need not bother any longer to compete in the Olympic Games. The soldiers have hurled hand-grenades, javelins and the corpus delicti so constantly that in discus-throwing, shot-putting and ordinary grappling they will be far superior to our pampered athletes. In the foot races they will also excel, because of the races they have run in all directions; and they have jumped over so many parapets that they must also be conceded the hurdles far in advance. Bracing air and life in the open have made lungs more leathery, the will stronger, the cranium more free of mental cobwebs.

While snow has tipped the mountain peaks continuously, the plains have likewise had cool currents. Wherever the opposing armies faced each other the air was heavy with frost; and one unwittingly compared the currents with the drafts which sweep through the assembly hall of a bankers' convention or any bank president's office on loan application day.

CHAPTER XIX

ON THE PRESS AND THE GULLIBLE PUBLIC

EARLY in the war the press bureaus of the various countries were brought to the highest point of efficiency. The Kaiser's press bureau was undoubtedly as efficient as the bureaus situated at Paris, London and Petrograd, but its product must first pass through enemy hands and be edited according to the rules of the International Board of Censorship. It did not always get to the gullible public in its original form, and was frequently deleted altogether. The Kaiser's bureau, for instance, told repeatedly how his armies were stepping all over the contorted face of Europe, but the Allied censors wrote so much between the lines that the sense of the thing was destroyed absolutely. In other words, the Allies were winning most of their victories on paper, while the Germans were winning theirs on the battle-field.

The advantage that the Germans enjoyed lay in the fact that they had a more tactical position geographically. While the Kaiser's heroes were hunching from center toward circumference, the Allies were pressing hard from the circumference toward the center. Naturally the Germans were more nimble in flitting here and there with their prize fighting units, while the Allies must travel à la Burton Holmes half-way around the world to make it from one theater to another.

But we are digressing sadly. The biggest yarns of all are said to have passed through Constantinople and Petrograd, where translations of Balzac, Munchausen and Jules Verne caused the minds of the writers to wander badly. In slack times the war correspondents related tales of atrocities sworn to before a notary public. Neutral nations were inexpressibly shocked and soon became convinced that the Dark Ages had returned, intensified with darkness of the Stygian variety. The lay reader set it down in his mind that Attila the Hun was the personification of milky human kindness when compared with the savage warrior of the twentieth century, and that the most ruthless Ancient Crusader was really unworthy of the name of chief.

Although a number of American war correspondents remained at home in order to give quicker service, most of them actually went to the front, and so did the movie men and the still-life photographers. Writers who had mastered Italian and French curse words and salutations in downtown New York restaurants and had picked up stray German phrases in Kaegebein's Hoboken froth shop naturally had the best chance to get along abroad.

An enterprising correspondent who was denied admission to the German lines hid in a powder

"My grand-dad played an oboe," the correspondent said.

barrel and was transported in due time to the front. He was in a dilemma as to how to get out quietly, until a soldier helped him by lighting a pipe too near. As the smoke cleared away and the correspondent removed the débris from his eye, the commanding general rushed up and demanded passports, resting a sword heavily on the correspondent's neck as he did so.

"What is your name?" shouted the commander.

"Eddie Ranck, of the moonshine district of Kentucky; author of 'The Night Rider' and other popular plays and fiction. I offer a letter of introduction from William Jennings Bryan."

"Bryan's signature is no good over here."

"Then I offer a letter from Johannus Daniels."

"That leg-o'-mutton sailor? Bah! Corporal, summon the firing squad."

"Be reasonable, Major; you forget that I am due some consideration. My grandfather once played an oboe in a German band and often delighted the Kaiser."

"Now you are getting somewhere," the commander admitted. "The corporal will countermand the order and bring the gentleman a uniform, gun and helmet. The Kaiser will be delighted to know that the grandson of an old friend is fighting fiercely for him!"

CHAPTER XX

GRAVE CONCERN IN AMERICA

TWO of the most important events of the spring of 1915 were the unhorsing of the wretched Secretary of State and the sinking of Elbert Hubbard, Alfy Vanderbilt, several Yale and Harvard men and a thousand foreigners on a giant liner bound for Liverpool. The ship referred to was steaming near her port of destination when she bumped into one of the biggest torpedoes the Germans had in stock, and listed to starboard at once. Passengers rushed for the life-boats, the end-seat hogs getting there first; but heroes gave their seats to the ladies. These heroes sank without a murmur and will also go down in deep-sea lore.

Many telegrams from around the country were sent to Washington praying that something be done, and the President announced that the Kaiser would be held to a strict accountability. The President also sent for the Secretary of State, who came in such haste that he left his collar and one shoe behind.

"Will you kindly sign another note?" anxiously inquired the President, getting straight down to business. "The Kaiser has sunk some more of our leading citizens."

"You don't say so!" exclaimed the astonished Secretary.

"I do," said the President. "We must record a protest without delay."

While the President put on the finishing touches the Secretary scratched on a pad with an indelible pencil; and occasionally the Secretary bit the end of the pencil and sighed like a grampus. Finally the note was ready, the Secretary signed it and limped back to his hotel.

The Kaiser caught a taxicab at the front when he heard the note was on the way, and broke all speed records to Berlin to receive it. He denied every charge, and couched his answers in language that was none too polite. More notes were exchanged and the recovered victims were laid tenderly away.

Mexico seized the opportunity to rise up again and was treated to condign punishment in the shape of another warning note. Altogether, it was the most noteworthy period in the history of the United States. Many people clamored for an opportunity to defend the country's honor, many preferred a skirmish with the Mexicans as a sincere forward step in the Preparedness Program which the Democrats had been talking about, and others did not want war with anybody. The Republicans, being sadly in the minority in Congress, maintained silence. Thinking persons with no dwarfing political ties declared that they would rather fight now than put horrible wars on posterity.

"God bless you!" they exclaimed in the same breath.

A lapse of time cooled temporarily the country's anger as to the Kaiser, but after a while another ship carrying valuable American lives was sunk, and this proved the last straw. The President called his long-faced Cabinet together, and also summoned the Secretary.

"I know just what you are going to say," asserted the Secretary, his temperature rising several calories. "You really must excuse me. Can I serve you in any other way?"

"Yes," replied the President; "take your desk back to Nebraska with you."

"How about the hat-rack?"

"Does that belong to you?"

"Yes; business is business."

"Well, take it along; but before you go, I want to thank you for what you did for me at Baltimore."

"Oh, don't mention it."

"God bless you!"

"God bless you, too!"

CHAPTER XXI

MR. FORD'S OCEAN JOY-RIDE

WE shall now proceed to chronicle a unique voyage which well-meaning citizens of the United States undertook in order that the soldier boys might quit the trenches by Christmas time and return to their weepy families.

The voyage depended mostly on the person and pocket-book of Hennery Ford, who had succeeded in the automobile business and was more than well off. Plainly speaking, Mr. Ford had the dough, and he made it himself out of a simple idea. Had he been a poorer spender than he was an advertiser it is doubtful if he could have enlisted a corporal's guard to take the good ship Oscar II to Europe and compel the rulers to cease fighting each other. Under the circumstances, however, the advocates of peace flocked to his side and held the banner high.

The Kaiser was suspicious of the voyage and the voyagers and so expressed himself. King George warned the party in advance that the warmest reception would probably be found in the frigid zone, paradoxical as it might seem. But all of the icebergs in Baffin's Bay would have been insufficient to cool the ardor of the gay company over the prospect of a brilliant success in such a noble enterprise.

The sailing point was Hoboken, a village of hyphens noted for its harbor, its dark beer fountains, its little German bands on every corner, its Swiss-cheese sandwiches and its Stevens Institute of Technology. Conditions for the voyage were ideal, and the scenes at the pier, where many anxious people stood, craved description. Some could hardly contain themselves, they were so hysterically happy. A messenger brought a pair of gray squirrels as mascots for the party.

The former Secretary of State waved a fond farewell with a bandanna handkerchief, and an old woman rushed over and kissed him loudly on the hand. Mr. Ford stood like a marble statue on the prow of the ship. Presently he raised a wicked-looking drink. Keep your seat, gentle reader,—it was only a coca-cola! The passengers started singing sacred hymns and shouting, and a great cheer went up from the docks. The excitement was so dramatically intense that a nut lost his balance and fell overboard, and nobody had presence of mind enough to send a squirrel to the rescue.

All of the guests were unqualifiedly in favor of peace, but before the ship had quit Sandy Hook differences of opinion arose as to how to get it. One faction favored steaming to The Hague with peace proposals, while the others wanted to go straight to the Kaiser. The split in the congregation widened, and as a compromise the ship was

The good ship Oscar set sail in a worthy cause.

headed for Christiania, in Norway. Hearing a great hubbub at the city pier, Mr. Ford sent for a messenger and said:

"Messenger, tell me truly: What are the good people cheering about?"

"Did you say *cheering*, sir?"

"That's what I said."

"I will gladly go overboard if the people are not *jeering*, sir."

The peace leader fell heavily into a steamer chair and the third cook rushed him a drink of hot lemonade. Mr. Ford could not stand the cold shoulder that way. He came to shortly, but will never look the same. He told the skipper to flounder around the ocean and he would foot the bills, and then he went back to the land of his birth to scrutinize his factory sales lists and build himself up.

The bill for the voyage was nigh four hundred thousand dollars, which Mr. Ford declared was more than he had ever paid for a joy-ride on land, but was well worth the price, seeing as how he had done his durndest for peace and had got mentioned for the presidency.

CHAPTER XXII

MARKING TIME AT SALONIKI

WHAT was the Kaiser doing to amuse himself all this time? He had captured all the territory in Europe that did not have too great an Allied army population, and now he ran a steamroller through Serbia so as to get into closer communication with the Sultan and his clan. The Serb army and King Peter retreated through the mountain passes as fast as possible and wound up at island hiding-places and Saloniki, where the Gallipoli remnant of the British army had landed, together with a large number of the brave French.

Nobody could stop the redoubtable Kaiser, and for a time things looked very blue for the Allies at the Greek port. Each Prussian soldier apparently could get up as much momentum on short notice as a freight car moving downhill with a load of hardwood lumber. Even the Greek life insurance companies were afraid, and would insure Allied soldiers only in the principal sum of $41 for a yearly premium of $24.95. This was before Serbia collapsed, and now the officials of the companies quit the game and reinvested the funds in a string of hat-cleaning and shoe-shining parlors and banana-stands. From the last reports they were doing a large business with the soldier boys.

"I'm proud of my noble army!" sobbed the King.

Just as it appeared the Germans and Bulgars would launch a fierce attack and try to precipitate their enemies into the sea, word came that they would do no such thing. Pressed for a statement, the Kaiser replied, "We have other mullet to fry." Investigation disclosed that the Kaiser had left the Bulgars to attack the Allies, and had moved his own troops to other fronts to help hard-pressed comrades. The Kaiser fully expected his wishes to be carried out, but the Bulgar King got cold feet at the last moment and backed down.

Prior to quitting this theater the Kaiser threw a handful of troops into Montenegro to extend his dominions a bit farther, and these troops began a hot pursuit of the venerable King, who sought refuge in the crags. The King vowed that he would never surrender or die with his boots under a bed. Summoning his army at dusk, he delivered an impassioned, tearful address.

"The monarch does not wear pants that can catch me!" shrieked the sadly distraught King as his army divided the last allotment of pease and bread. "We must fight on until we realize our national ideals! Do you hear me, Corporal? Do you hear me, Private?"

CHAPTER XXIII

BIRD'S-EYE VIEW OF VERDUN

THE Battle of Verdun began early in 1916 and will probably last until the Platinum Age. It was a titanic battle composed of a large number of monster battles and smaller battles. Our purpose shall be to present only a hint of what Verdun was, for it is well-nigh impossible in a work of this size to do the conflict justice. Other historical works will doubtless go more into detail, but for these the public must wait a great while, in the opinion of the long-whiskered soothsayers and prophets.

The Kaiser suddenly started a monster offensive drive to annex a sleepy little town in northern France and to throw General Joffre's army into an immense cave. Just how the Kaiser expected this coup to end the war is not quite clear, but he evidently had his reasons. And he based a frantic appeal to his men on the ground that he and the Crown Prince soon would celebrate their birthdays and they wished Verdun for a birthday present. The Crown Prince's natal day followed that of the Kaiser, so if the father's ruse failed to work, perhaps the son's would. Let us view the battle as it progressed on the birthday of the Kaiser.

When the Germans started the Battle of Verdun

they created something that made Satan's and Dante's celebrated infernos look like an ordinary furnace in a second-rate locomotive works. Countless Germans scampered from caves and dug-outs like a lot of prairie dogs venturing forth to devour a fallen ant-bear. As soon as the whites of their eyes were visible, the Allies blazed away and felled a huge number.

The din was positively frightful, the heat intense, but the Kaiser's braves with heroic self-sacrifice hurled themselves into the holocaust. The French mowed them down with machine guns, the English peppered them with slender bullets, the East Indians harried them with bolos, and the native colored citizens of Africa lifted their helmets with well-directed boomerangs. A fair percentage of the Germans were bald and they suffered terribly from exposure. The whiskers of the Landsturm were shot away entirely, but they (the Landsturm) pressed valiantly to the front.

No less than 100,000, at a conservative estimate, became entangled in Allied barb-wire made in the United States. They behaved very curiously as the Allies prodded them from one side and their comrades urged them forward from the other. On the left wing the Germans succeeded in capturing a valuable position, consisting of a high knoll and a frog-pond. But they were driven out in a furious counter-attack, and left much freight for the enemy to care for.

The most pluperfect excitement probably existed

The battle of Verdun was a very chaotic affair.

in the center. It was the old story of the irresist-
ible force hitting the immovable mass. Sparks flew
so high that Vulcan must have accepted the challenge and belabored his battered anvil ferociously.
The noise was so deafening and disconcerting that
a French sentry who had stuck to his post a week
without relief now found it impossible to sleep a
wink. A perfectly frigid winter morning had been
transformed in a few minutes into a climate that
many a perspiring trooper called as hot as the en-
gine-room of a tropical liner in the middle of July.
The only personage needed to make the scene more
intensely realistic was Satan himself, and he was
ably represented by the Kaiser.

Shells snipped off the mighty oaks like scythes in
a bed of young asparagus. Aviators fought des-
perately in the air and fell with crushing force on
fat old generals below. The Germans presently
began to hurl hand-grenades into the teeth of the
enemy, and the enemy countered with iron missiles
against their diaphragms. The game was plainly
one of flesh against steel, and the metal was beginning to break down many an iron constitution.
Judged by the results, football could no longer be
called the king of devastating sports.

A detachment of cavalry was sent into the writhing vortex to contribute its mite to the sum total.
The brave horsemen crumpled up like a thin sliver
of celluloid in the blaze of a blast-furnace, and they
never could rise again. Words now fail us, gentle
reader, so we shall return to the side of the Kaiser.

The Kaiser had watched the engagement from a vantage-point a short distance away, and the valor of his warriors was certainly enough to atone for the enormous price of the birthday celebration. Surely it was a tribute that few could enjoy, and the Kaiser was in an appreciative, philosophical frame of mind when approached during a lull at dusk by a tattered general.

"Our troops fought like madmen; why do you suppose we did not capture more enemy positions?" queried the general as he dropped his telescope.

"That is one of the things I shall eventually ask St. Peter," responded the Kaiser.

CHAPTER XXIV

ARMLESS RUSSIANS COME BACK

FOR two weary years the Czar's men were forced to fight without any arms, but their legs were good and that explains how Russian civilization has been saved to mankind, and how the Czar's millions have staged the most gratifying come-back on record.

When the Czar started marching his hordes into Germany he very wisely put all the bone-heads in the front rank with the jail-birds, and several millions of these fell into the Kaiser's hands and have been haunting him ever since. The quick wits of the army, seeing the serious predicament, decided to march back home and get things to fight with. This explains the great retreat of 4,000,000 peasants before von Hindenburg, and in no other way can it be explained. Events proved that the Russians needn't have done that spectacular cross-country hike if the creature Circumstance had not jinxed them. The Russian army was most glorious in retreat, for it maintained its autonomy, although it lost a considerable part of its anatomy.

Recalling the past, the Kaiser refused to be led into the Moscow trap that caused the downfall of Napoleon, but camped in the fertile valleys of the

"Come out of that swamp and fight!" yelled the Kaiser.

temperate zone. He dared the Czar to come out of the swamps and fight, but for a long time the challenge was not accepted. The Czar had made another engagement. He was going southward to punish the Turks for their inconsiderate treatment of the Armenians. The Czar also wanted to break up the Sultan's harem, so he smote him on the hip and cleft him through the scabbard. In a remarkably short time the Czar captured Erzerum and 100,000 hungry Turks, with a quantity of arms and ammunition; but the Sultan swore the place had been deserted and a handful of howling dervishes were the only booty. Readers accustomed to devour war topics searched for Erzerum on the war maps, but had no success, as usual.

After this stroke the Czar swept through parts of Austria and took charge of half a million dopy Austrians, causing the world to sit up and gasp. Things were truly breaking well with him, but the same could not be said for the British near Bagdad, one of the Sultan's strongholds. Aided by floods, the eager Turks hemmed up a force at Kut-el-Amara. Thousands of clamorous Moslems surrounded the marooners several weeks, and when the enemy had been reduced to acorns, tallow candles, rawhide and sponges, the general in charge threw up the last-named article.

CHAPTER XXV

INTERVIEW WITH THE KAISER

IN this chapter we present a formal interview with the Kaiser which we believe to be the only authorized and genuine statement he has made to a foreign correspondent since the war began. The Kaiser insisted on dictating his answers through the royal stenographer, saying he had often been made to stand for things he had never said. The result follows:

Q.—Your Majesty, who started this war, anyway?
A.—I don't know; I didn't do it.
Q.—Do you think you have a good chance of winning?
A.—There can be no doubt about it.
Q.—On what do you base your belief?
A.—I base my belief on the fact that my victorious army is unconquered and can never be crushed.
Q.—Is there any truth in the report that food riots have shaken Berlin?
A.—No truth whatever.
Q.—Then the food question is not worrying you?
A.—Not so you could notice it.
Q.—How many men have you in the field?
A.—I cannot answer that off-hand.

Picture of the Kaiser submitting to an interview.

Q.—How about their equipment?

A.—It is excellent.

Q.—How about the report that you are running short of gunpowder and poison gases?

A.—Nothing in it. Our natural resources are wonderful. Our men of science have new processes.

Q.—How much money does the government owe the people?

A.—Considerable.

Q.—Will it ever be paid back?

A.—Its return will not be asked. The government protects the people, and they fight for it and give up their money.

Q.—How do you figure on beating the Allies?

A.—Russia will be forced into a separate peace. Von Hindenburg is after them again.

Q.—How long is this war going to last?

A.—If I knew that I wouldn't tell it around.

Q.—As long as the Hundred Years' War?

A.—Perhaps.

Q.—How about your submarine policy?

A.—That is too general a question.

Q.—Do you expect to return to the old practices?

A.—Very likely.

Q.—When will the German navy make its stand against the English?

A.—I cannot answer that question. It will be a good scrap.

Q.—Is it true that the German people are using soap cakes?

A.—I think my good people use soap cakes every
Saturday night. .

Q.—How is your supply of beer?

A.—Tip-top. We seldom drink water.

Q.—What is your opinion of prohibition?

A.—I don't understand you.

Q.—What do you think of cutting out near-beer?

A.—Near-beer is harmful. You should use the old
style.

Q.—Have you ever met Mr. Bryan?

A.—I think I heard him speak once.

Q.—Is he an orator or a statesman?

A.—He is a spread-eagle orator. It would take
Monk Halsey to advertise him properly.

Q.—What do you think of Secretary Daniels?

A.—Punk! He couldn't scale a military mast for
a thousand dollars.

Q.—Didn't he get a real navy for the American
people?

A.—The American people forced him into it. Look
up the record.

Q.—Who is the strongest man in the Cabinet?

A.—Garrison. The rest are not worth a continen-
tal.

Q.—Didn't you hear that Garrison resigned?

A.—The hell you say! They put a dry-goods mer-
chant in his place, maybe.

Q.—No, a tennis-player. Who is going to be the
next President?

A.—I can't think of his name. He's the animated
feather-duster, and he ought to sweep the

country. He and I are sure winners, if you want to make a side bet.

Q.—Do you believe in woman's suffrage?

A.—After the war I may be obliged to.

Q.—Are you in favor of early marriages?

A.—Early in peace times, often in war.

Q.—To what do you attribute your success in life?

A.—I make ''Wills'' out of my ''Musts,''—that's all.

CHAPTER XXVI

THE KAISER'S FLEET VENTURES FORTH

THE outstanding feature of the spring of 1916 was a great naval tie-up between the Germans and the English, which resulted in a splendid victory for each, judging by the claims of the respective sides.

The battle raged many hours, from the coast of Norway to the Kiel Canal, and was witnessed by numerous ·island natives from the tops of palm trees. German scouts patrolling the coast were engaged by an advance unit of the main English fleet. The prize part of the Kaiser's navy steamed up and pumped a great deal of wrought-iron into the smaller enemy ships. The English wireless sputtered calls for help, and Admiral Jellyfish, an old tar with a real fleet, dashed to the rescue.

Frightful noises arose everywhere and the sea was lashed into a mad mass of soapy foam. More noise was heard than it is possible to generate in a mammoth American boiler factory where half the force is hammering steel plate with forty-pound sledges and the other half thoughtlessly chucking monkey wrenches and crow-bars into the works. This very commotion, according to authorities (Professor Snider, Professor Hurtel and old Dr.

The enemy suffered bitter defeat in the North Sea.

Glass), drove Europe's sharks to the shores of the United States, with regrettable disasters.

Many of the inferior English ships were shot to pieces, but when Admiral Jellyfish arrived he retaliated in goodly measure. Nearly as many ships were sunk as repose in the American navy, and since both sides chalked up a victory, it must have been as dazzling a spectacle as Paine's pyrotechnics at a world's fair.

An immeasurably greater loss to England, however, was the unexpected sinking a short time later of Lord Kitchener, the adored military official. Kitchener was not a very large man, but he was as big as men ever get to be. He was possessed of an iron will and an eagle eye that gained him many victories. He never married, but in spite of that fact climbed as high on the ladder as any married man, and was the idol of bachelors everywhere. He was undoubtedly as happy as a single man can be.

Kitchener died with his medals on as well as his boots, and, luckily, before encountering any glum anti-climax, with which so many great old men are doomed to wrestle. He had not quite hit the autumn of life, and had he lived there is no telling what would have happened to the Germans.

CHAPTER XXVII

KING ALBERT'S WARNING

"I HAVE not been so busy with the war that I could not notice some things that have taken place in America," King Albert confided to our correspondent in a remarkable interview which is presented exclusively herewith.

"You see, I am quite a reader of the newspapers, and while I don't believe every word I read, I manage to keep pretty well posted. I have always been a good friend to Uncle Sam and I want to send him a message which I believe he will be interested to hear. Just take down what I say, word for word.

"Uncle Sam is living in the worst fools' paradise I ever heard of! He imagines, like the ostrich, that as long as his head is in the sand he is safe. Not so! Didn't I have the same feeling once upon a time? And now my beautiful country is a barren waste and a big pile of debris; and my good people have been driven hither and thither and no longer have any homes.

"Prior to the outbreak of this war I would have laughed at the man who would have told me anybody might overrun my realm. Just look at me now,—I am lucky to have a hay-stack to sleep on and three squares a day!"

Von Hindenburg.
A Uhlan cavalryman.

A Scotch bagpiper.
The King of Rumania.

"How do you figure there is any danger?" our correspondent ventured to ask. "Haven't we appropriated more than half a billion for battle-ships and submarines?"

"True, young man," replied King Albert, "but there is a difference between appropriating money and spending it. I offer it as my honest opinion that that appropriation will not be exhausted before you are an old man—unless, of course, some power throws big shells into your principal coast cities. And then it will be too late."

"Who is there to attack us?"

"I cannot tell you that, any more than I could name the footpad who one of these dark nights will take your roll. But just consider the situation: Japan is double-taxing her citizens to wipe out her war debts and put her on a financial footing with creditor nations. She is waxing fat from munitions profits, which go to the government rather than to individuals. In every way she is helping Russia in the war, and before long she will call on Russia to reciprocate. A coalition between Russia and Japan is just as possible as an alliance between France and Russia, or between England and Italy."

"But the new Japanese premier says he will not unsheathe the sword," prompted our correspondent hopefully and rather sophomorically.

"My friend, you make me laugh! Don't you know that every ruler since Rufus the Redbeard has given expression to the same sentiment? Uncle

King Albert forgot himself and heaved a shoe.

Sam is a fine fish if he doesn't take that with a large grain of salt! You notice the Jap statesman hints that Japan has a destiny to work out and that she will let nothing stand in the way. Very well, —that nullifies the effect of the assurance. Amid the din and clatter that occupies all Europe, Japan is giving China periodic injections of dope, and in a short time she will apply the chloroform. She will next move toward your white elephant—the Philippines—and then toward another rich·prize— the Hawaiian Islands—and perhaps Mexico will be the open door to Japan to settle on the North American continent.''

"General Carranza assures us he will not let the Japs get a·foothold,'' declared our correspondent, still unconvinced.

"Ah, my dear fellow, General Carranza is a fly-by-night ruler. He is long on whiskers and wisdom, but some things he cannot foretell. And he cannot side-step the Grim Reaper. A new leader will rise out of Mexico's chaos. For that matter, Uncle Sam needs Mexico and the little Tabasco Sauce countries all the way to the Panama Canal. 'South American Friendship' is a fine sentiment, but it leads to nowhere in particular. Then if you really want to act the big brother and do something for humanity, you should go into Mexico and clean it up. Is there one who will gainsay that a Mexico under the American flag would be worse off in any particular than it is now? I can't see it for dust!''

King Albert leaned back in his chair and heaved

a long sigh. Then he lit another Turkish cigarette and continued:

"In my odd moments I keep up pretty well with affairs in America. I know who won out in the recent election, and I know that Tammany Hall lost a lot of its voting strength in New York City, and I know that Yale beat both Princeton and Harvard this fall at football. I have a friend in New Jersey who writes me confidentially that your National Guard will pass out of existence in 1922 under the provisions of your Hay bill. He says your war chief doesn't know enough to acknowledge a military salute. Suppose the Kaiser should win this war—where would you be? Japan to the west of you, Mexico to the south of you, Germany to the east of you, the anti-military party inside of you— what in the world would become of you? On top of that you have only broomsticks to fight with, and you have little more than enough powder to blow off a small boy's hat! Don't be deceived by the gyrations along the Mexican border! The mob and the politicians are conspiring to sell you into slavery! Uncle Sam is no longer the spindle-legged Cassius with the Adam's-apple neck who fights for honor and for home! My friend, Uncle Sam is a flabby something which is bigger around the waist than around the chest!"

"What in the world are we to do?" wailed our disconsolate correspondent.

"Get an ounce of preparedness and avoid the pound of woe," suggested King Albert. "Turn a deaf ear to the platitudes of the politicians. Throw Uncle Sam overboard and set you up an old-fashioned king."

"How about presidents for the Europeans?" shouted our correspondent, as a new idea struck him.

"Get to hell out of here!" shrieked the Belgian king. And the king heaved a shoe that whizzed dangerously close to our correspondent's head.

CHAPTER XXVIII

ESSAY ON THE GREAT CATACOMBS

EUROPE'S geographical countenance is not the pastoral scene that it used to be. It is rough on the surface with excrescences, and beneath the surface it is a network of great catacombs with which the ancient variety are not to be mentioned in the same breath. Unless the traveler is possessed of excellent poise, he had better not try to roam around Europe on a dark night. The native citizen who knows the ground fairly well has tried it with disastrous results. The native either breaks his neck or loses his last collar button, which is nearly as bad. He never sues the municipality, however; he might get a judgment, but he would never collect the money.

Europeans are freely predicting that when some of the experiences of the soldiers are related we shall hear no more about the Black Hole of Calcutta except as a summer resort; also that when the veterans of Time's Most Spectacular War whittle on their peg-legs at the corner grocery and grow reminiscent, the veterans of all other wars will dive through the back door and seek whatever cover is in sight.

Europe's catacombs will not bring a high price

for farming purposes or real estate subdivisions at the close of hostilities, but a plan is already under way whereby capitalists will build a subway system that will be a marvel to the world.

Real estate men also see an advantage in so much frantic digging. Whenever a client wants to erect a skyscraper, he can get a corner lot with a natural basement; and ghosts that live on the premises will see that tenants do not burn electric lights later than nine o'clock at night.

CHAPTER XXIX

AS WE GO TO PRESS

THE Battle of the Somme was started by the British to relieve the weary French at Verdun, and undoubtedly did a great deal in that direction. It was staged west of Verdun and served to keep the Kaiser hopping from one theater of war to the other with great dexterity.

The Somme fighting was very much like the rest, except that the English were on the offensive, and for a description of a typical engagement we refer our readers to a previous chapter on our glimpse of Verdun. A decided feature of the Somme advances was the unparalleled heroism of the Scotch as they marched forth behind pied bagpipemen to a glorious end. The Irish marched behind briar pipes and were no less courageous.

Disappointment was keen among many persons here and there as the Kaiser failed to blow up after the Allied offensive had been in progress some time on all the fronts. Eventually the opposing troops settled down to the humdrum of every-day trench existence and prepared for another Christmas and winter of watchful waiting, punctuated with occasional sorties when the mercury jumped up. Camp-followers were reported joining the armies in large

Snapshots from a battlefield.

numbers, having found loot and a living unusually hard to connect with any longer.

The fretful King of Rumania finally entered the war with the Allies to recover territory wrested from him by the Austrians in the Stone Age, and Italy declared war on the Kaiser and agreed to march in the final procession on Berlin. Greece started helping the Allies informally, but officially executed a Balkan Hesitation that is without parallel. Greece and Rumania are the war barometers of Europe. They generally indicate which way the winds are blowing; but of course all prophets have their off-days. For particulars, consult the King of Rumania, who went into the struggle as the Balance of Power and soon became the Goat.

The Allies rushed to cut off the Turks and the Bulgars from the Germans and to give Austria a fatal punch. Nothing could please the Kaiser better, in our opinion, because he has been propping up tottering helpers to the detriment of his own game.

As we go to press, comparative quiet reigns on all the fronts. Our wide-awake correspondent cables that the French captured a German birdman and searched him for documents which it was believed would tell of a plan for the Kaiser to abdicate. All that the searchers found, however, were a compass and some cigarette papers.

KILLJOYS ON HELGOLAND

(IF THE KAISER SHOULD WIN)

ON a lonely isle which the natives knew
    By the name of Helgoland,
In a year we don't remember sat
A wretched little band
Of ginks whom the layman might suspect
Were strangers in those parts:
All garbed in robes of somber hue,
With cross-bones o'er their hearts.

"Call de roll!" a stocky Prussian yelled—
  ('Twas the Corporal of the Guard);
"Ya, ya!!" the Adjutant replied,
  And he called them good and hard:
"Kink Georch, standt hup! I vill tell you vot
  De Kaiser says to do:
You take dis pick und dig, und dig,
  Till you've digged de earth clean through!

"Czar Nicholas of Petersburg,
  Standt hup,—how dare you schleep!
Der vay your chin hangs on your chest
  Vould make der anchels veep!
You iss to bear dis ball und chain

A wretched little band languished on Helgoland.

Mit your royal ankle,—so,
Und trodt der island all aroundt,—
On your mark, gedt ready,—go!

"Der Bresident of France—vere's he?
Addention! Can't you hear?
You iss to shovel coal a vile
For der ships down at der pier!
Kink Victor, take dis sledge-hammer,
Und mit dot rock pile tussle;
Go easy for a day or two—
Don't strain your royal muscle!

"Und vere iss Peter, Kink of Serbs?—
He needn't hide from me!—
I'll make Kink Peter Cheese Police
Mit der islanders,—hee, hee!!
Iss der Kink of Montenegro hier?
Vell, he must do hees bit;
To push a peanut aroundt der fort
Mit de endt of hees nose iss it!

"Kink Albert, he's a brave younk man,—
He fights in storm und fog;
Der easy chob for der Belgian Kink,—
He keeps der island's log!
If dere's any more dot ain't been calldt,
Chust let heem raise hees hand;
Der Kaiser vould be proud if he
Could see hees little band!

[120]

"Now let's all get to vurrk at vonce,
  Und no man yell, 'Calf rope!'
A day iss twenty-four hours, my mates,
  Und der sun vill shine, I hope!
In a hundert years I vill come again,
  Midt medals for each of you,
Providet you're villin' I chudge in full
  Py der manner of vurrk you do!''

"One minute, chief!" said the good King George,
"Before I start to dig
  To China from Helgoland I'd like
  Some mittens, soft and big!"
"Yes, chief, and I have a last request,"
  Piped the stocky King of France,—
"Inasmuch as I'm going to shovel coal,
  I'd like some suitable pants."

"My wants are simple, mark you well,"
  To the Adjutant quoth the Czar;
"When you stop at the store I wish you'd bring
  A good five-cent cigar."
"When I left home I told the Pope
  I would write him now and then;
Would you be so kind," King Victor asked,
"As to bring me a fountain pen?"

The Montenegrin King, in truth,
  Was on his hands and knees;
"I'm getting the lay of the land," he said,—
"Will you haul me a peanut, please?"

King Albert asked for a writing-pad,
The King of the Serbs for some water;
"I'm sorry, Peter," the guard replied,
"But dringks are two for a quarter."

King Peter surrendered his last luck-piece,
And the mercenary Adjutant flew
To the shore with a vessel and back real quick,
(For the king was thirsty and blue);
"This water is salt!" the King did shriek,—
"To kill you dead I am due to!"
"Just hold your horses," the guard replied,—
"The quarter you gave me is pewter!"

The guard now ducked to devour his lunch,
And King George was feeling tired,
So the King sat down to collect his thoughts
At the risk of his getting fired.
"Frenchy," he said, "I will swap with you,—
As a miner I'm not any good."
"Then you can't shovel coal!" was the hot reply,
"And I wouldn't exchange if I could!"

"I feel for you, Victor," the Czar opened up,
"I would fain bear your burden for you";
But King Victor was wise, and he solemnly said,
"Czar Nicholas, damned if you do!"
So they all fell to fighting as in days long ago,
(And alas! it was sad that they did!):
In a concreted dungeon they lit on their beans,
And the Adjutant clamped on the lid.

L'ENVOI

A century past, the Adjutant came,
And a tear made his eye truly sad,
For he felt in his heart that his unhappy crew
Had finally gotten in bad.
The Czar was all mildewed, and so were the
    rest,—
But of more it is useless to tell;
I wish I were sure which direction they took,—
To Heaven, to Halfway or Hell!